1000 SWEATERS

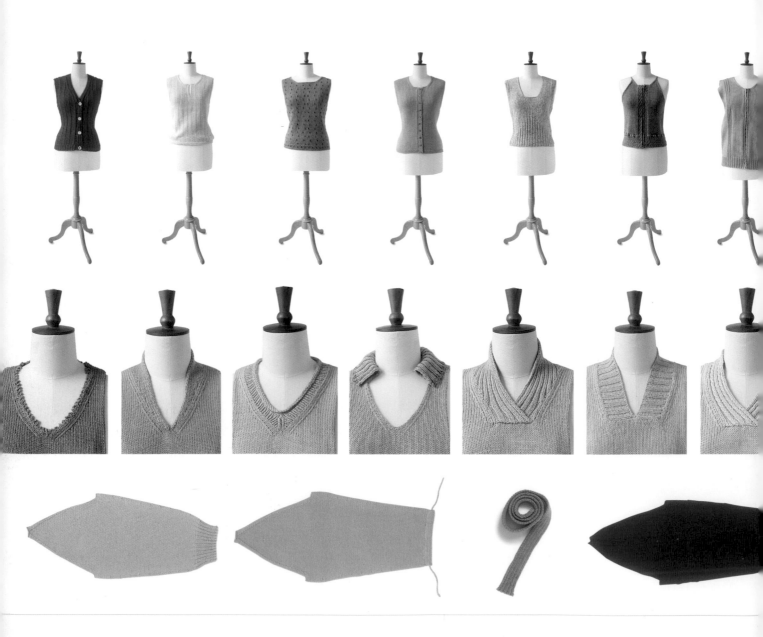

krause publications
An F&W Publications Company

1000 SWEATERS

MIX AND MATCH PATTERNS FOR THE PERFECT, PERSONALIZED SWEATER

AMANDA GRIFFITHS

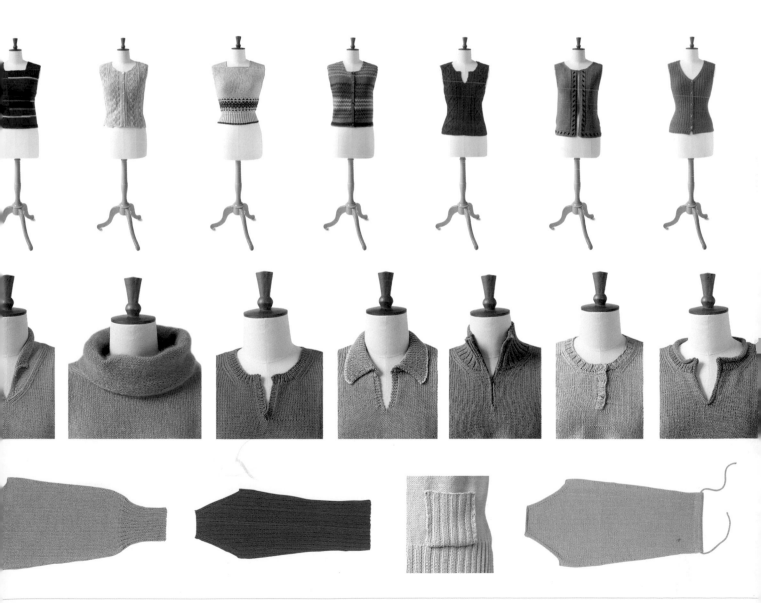

A QUARTO BOOK

First published in North America in 2004
by Krause Publications
700 East State Street
Iola, WI 54990-0001

Library of Congress Catalog Card No
2003108026

ISBN 0-87349-716-3

QUAR.TSW

Conceived, designed, and produced by
Quarto Publishing plc
The Old Brewery
6 Blundell Street
London N7 9BH

Project editor Paula McMahon
Designer & art editor Elizabeth Healey
Illustrator Jennie Dooge
Photographer Jeff Cottenden
Pattern checker Pauline Hornsby
Text editor Anne Plume
Indexer Pamela Ellis
Assistant art director Penny Cobb

Art director Moira Clinch
Publisher Piers Spence

Manufactured by Pro-Vision Pte Ltd,
Singapore
Printed by Midas Printing International
Limited, China

CONTENTS

UPPER PAGES

LOWER PAGES

HOW TO USE THIS BOOK

More and more people are discovering handknitting as a rewarding and therapeutic craft. Knitting is a relaxing way to use spare time, and a great way to create desirable fashion garments that are unique.

1000 Sweaters gives you the opportunity to design and create your very own original garment to your own individual requirements.

This book acts as a manual for both new and experienced knitters, and aims to show you a range of design possibilities for a garment. Using the principle of mixing and matching pieces, a collection of body shells are provided to be combined with a range of necklines, sleeves, pockets, and belts. This system allows you to create unique and completely individual pieces, safe in the knowledge that each piece will fit together to create the garment of your choice.

MIX AND MATCHING THE PATTERNS

The body patterns are shown on the top part of the split page, and the additions—sleeve, neck, belt, and pocket variations—are shown on the lower part of the split page.

The body patterns are organized into three sections by armhole type—fitted sleeve, dropped sleeve, raglan sleeve—and are icon-coded to correspond with the appropriate sleeve in the bottom section to make selection as easy as possible.

DEGREE OF DIFFICULTY

all levels   *intermediate*   *advanced*

These symbols provide a guide to the degree of difficulty involved in each pattern and the level of experience that is required by the knitter.

ICONS USED IN THE BOOK

 Fitted sleeve   *Scoop neck*

 Dropped sleeve   *Square V-neck*

 Raglan sleeve   *Square neck*

 Crew neck   *Pocket*

 V-neck   *Belt*

Keyhole neck

CHECKLIST

1 Select your body shape.

2 Select the sleeve that fits the armhole of the body.

3 Select the neck design that fits the neck opening of the body.

4 Select any additional features, such as pockets or belts.

5 Decide on your trim detail, and check that it will work for all the component pieces you have selected, see page 8. Then note down any changes on the pattern so that you remember to include them when you are knitting.

6 Add up all the yarn requirements (the yardage total is very important, as this will determine how much yarn is required). Select your yarn, checking that it will give the look you want: see pages 126–7.

Materials

The yarn and equipment needed for each item are given at the beginning of the pattern. By changing the yarn you can create a different look, but be sure to use the same yarn to make each part of the sweater. See page 126 for advice on yarns.

Degree of difficulty

The wool symbols show how complex the pattern is.

Choosing a body

To select the body shape you want for your sweater, flip through the upper pages of the book

Gauge

The gauge, stated at the beginning of every pattern, is the same for every item, allowing you to mix and match to create the sweater of your choice. See page 9 for further advice on gauge.

Sizing guide

To create the sweater of your choice, you will need to knit all pieces to the same pattern size.

Choosing a sleeve

To select a sleeve design that will fit your garment, flip through the lower pages and match the sleeve icons

Rib and hem stitch

When designing your sweater, you must choose the same rib and hem stitch for the separate items. See page 8 for further advice.

Choosing a neck

To select a neck that will fit your sweater, flip through the lower pages and match the neck icons.

Charts

Cable and intarsia patterns have charts.

Choosing pockets and belts

If your sweater has a pocket or a belt icon, flip though the lower pages to find a choice of pockets and belts.

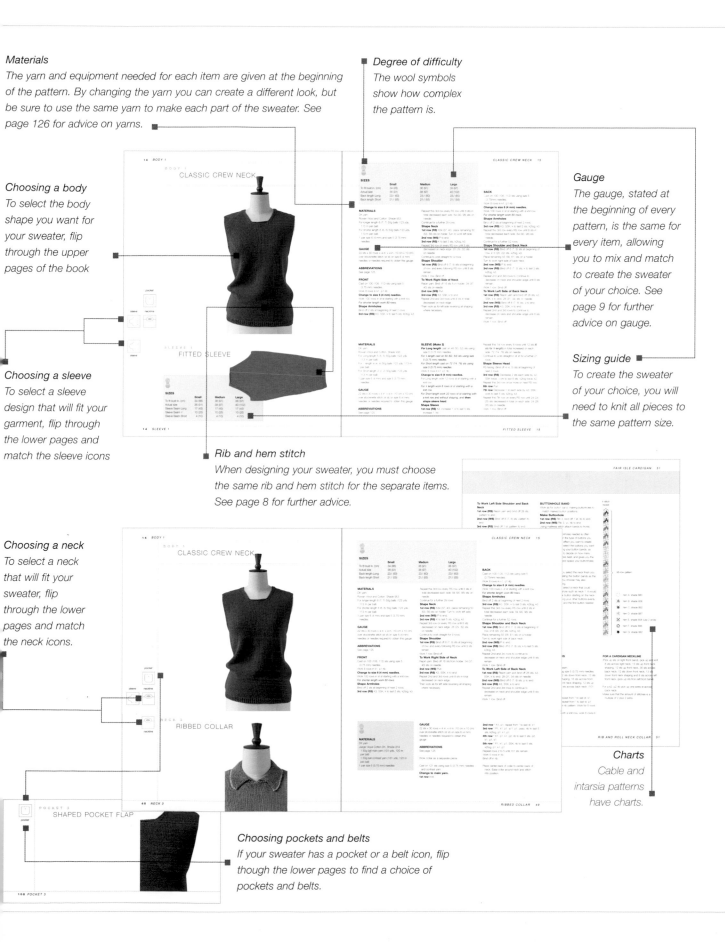

The Showcase section offers ideas and inspiration, for mix and matching to make your sweater.

Trims and stitch details must be consistent throughout the garment, so that your design looks balanced.

YARN

The designs featured have all been knitted in Rowan and Jaeger yarns. However, if you are unable to use the yarn quoted, there is a description of each yarn, its weight, length/yardage, and type in the pattern, so that you can find a substitute. For further information on the yarns used in the book, turn to page 126. All the projects have been designed using double knitting, or equivalent yarn type, which can all be knitted to the same gauge. Therefore all patterns can mix and match, and all yarns are interchangable, to create greater flexibility and choice.

SIZING

Each pattern gives a chest measurement with a small, medium, and large sizing. It also gives an actual size, or finished size, which indicates the fit of the garment if knitted to the correct gauge. The instructions for all the sizes are given throughout the pattern, starting with the smallest and the others in brackets. It is often useful to highlight the size you are working to before starting to knit to avoid any confusion. The patterns also include directions for different lengths of sleeves and body lengths so you have additional garment options.

CHANGING STITCHES FOR TRIMS AND DETAILS

You don't have to stick to the trim details specified in each pattern; you can use the pattern instructions from other projects for the garment you are knitting. However, it is important that you knit the same number of rows, and use the number of stitches stated in the pattern, as otherwise the length or width of the garment may be affected. Also make sure that trims and stitch details are consistent throughout the garment, so that your design looks considered and balanced. In the Showcase section, pages 114–123, some of the rib and hem details have been changed on the garments to demonstrate how to adapt a design.

BASIC SKILLS, CONSTRUCTION, AND ASSEMBLY

This section includes step-by-step illustrations to take you through the knitting basics and construction techniques to help you produce a successful garment and professional finish.

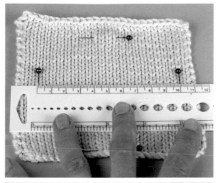

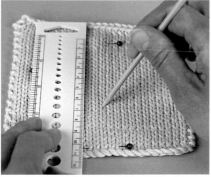

Measure the gauge by counting the stitches horizontally and the rows vertically.

Tip If gauge is tighter than recomended more yarn will be required to complete a garment, looser than specified and you'll have surplus yarn.

Gauge

All the patterns in this book are calculated using the same gauge: 22 stitches x 30 rows over 4 in. (10 cm) using stockinette stitch. This gauge is stated at the beginning of every pattern, and it is extremely important that you always work a gauge/stitch square before embarking on a whole garment in the yarn you have selected. The needles quoted on the pattern are only a suggested size, and you may need to use a different size needle to achieve the correct gauge. If your gauge is not the same as stated, then your garment will not match the sizing in the pattern and your garment will not fit properly.

How to measure gauge

Knit a swatch with the size of needles given in the instructions and using the yarn you have selected for your project. Add a few extra stitches and work a few more rows—26 stitches and 34 rows, for a gauge square of 22 stitches x 30 rows—because the edge stitches will be distorted. Gently press your swatch and place it flat on a surface.

Measure 4 in. (10 cm) across the square and mark with pins. Do the same vertically. If the number of stitches and rows is correct you know your finished garment will be the right size. If there are more stitches and rows, you are knitting too tightly, and your garment will be too small. Knit another swatch with larger needles. If there are too few stitches and rows, change to smaller needles and work another swatch and check again.

READING THE BALL BAND

When choosing your yarn, remember to check the information on the ball band. You should knit your garment with yarn from the same dye lot because different dye lots can vary in tone.

Gauge guide

Rowan Yarns
Holmfirth
England

SEE OVER FOR
ALTERNATIVE
CARE INSTRUCTIONS

22-24 sts
30-32 rows
10 cm/4 in

9-8
UK
5-6
US
3¼-4
mm

Needle size

ROWAN

wool cotton

Shade and dye lot

50% MERINO WOOL 50% COTTON
50% MERINO WOLLE 50% BAUMWOLLE
50% MERINO LAINE 50% COTTON

SH953   LOT5C2

5 013712 920028

Yarn content

In accordance with B.S. 984
Approx Length 113m (123 yds)

Yarn weight

50g

www.rowanyarns.co.uk

40° Warm (40° C) Wool Cycle,
minimum machine action

Cool iron

Do not bleach

P Dry clean in certain solvents

Do not tumble dry. Dry
flat out of direct sunlight

Care instructions

Pressing

Pressing your knitting before sewing up is an important stage in the construction process and will make an enormous difference to the finished garment. Always check the ball band for yarn care and test a sample first before applying heat to your finished knitting.

Pin each piece out to size with the wrong side facing you on a padded board, using a measure tape to check the measurements. Do not be tempted to skip this measuring stage. It can be alarming how much you can pull your knitting into the wrong shape without realizing it, and how much fabric can be steamed into the correct shape if required. Lay a dampened cotton muslin cloth on top of the knitted fabric, and gently apply the iron. Avoid stamping the iron too heavily or pushing it along the fabric surface. If the yarn is very delicate, or the fabric highly textured, pin out the pieces, dampen them with a water spray and allow them to dry naturally.

Construction

The construction process is generally the same for all the garments in this book. Any special instructions for specific projects will be mentioned in the pattern. Once the instructions for the neck attachment have been completed and both shoulder seams have been attached together, stitch the sleeves in place, and then stitch the side seams of the body and sleeves. Remember to check in the pattern if there are any turn-back cuffs or collars, as this may mean having to reverse the seams at some stage.

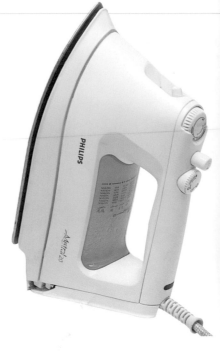

Mattress Stitch

1 It is important to get a neat edge when joining seams. To achieve this, lay both pieces out flat, with right sides facing and side edges vertical to each other. Thread a sewing needle with yarn and bring it through from the back as close to the bottom edge and side as possible. Make a figure-of-eight as illustrated. This gives a neat start to the seam.

2 Having taken the yarn through the right fabric piece, take the needle across and under the left piece of fabric and up through the same hole as the yarn, creating the figure-of-eight.

3 From the front, insert the needle into the side of the next stitch up on the right-hand side. Pointing the needle up, bring it through to the front, so that two bars of yarn lie across the needle.

4 Take the needle across to the left-hand side and insert it into the stitch that the last stitch left from. Pointing the needle up, bring it through to the front, two stitches up. Work like this from side to side, pulling up the stitches every 1 in. (2 cm) to tighten the seam.

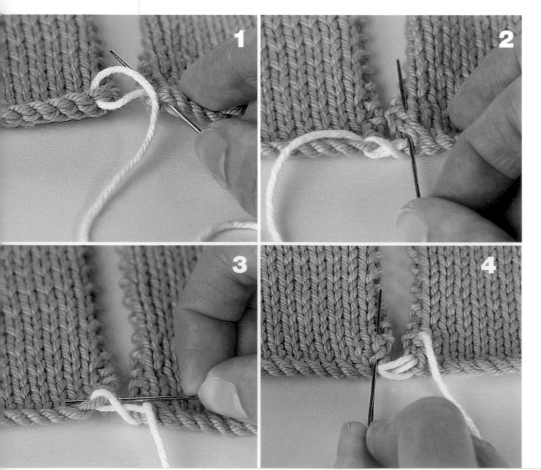

Joining the Sleeve to the Body with Mattress Stitch

1 When joining the sleeve to the body, mark the center of the sleeve with a pin, and match it up to the shoulder seam. Secure this central point with a stitch (or pin if you prefer). Do the same at the points where the sleeves meet the side edge of the armhole. This will help you to judge the gauge when sewing the pieces together.

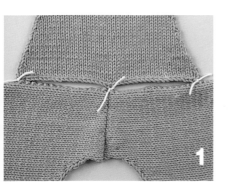

2 Following the instruction for mattress stitch, stitch in one stitch on the body, and as close to the bind-off edge as possible on the sleeve. Bring the sewing needle through the center of the edge stitch on the sleeve. From the front, insert the needle in between two stitches on the body and bring it through to the front of the work two bars up.

3 From the front, insert the needle back into the stitch on the sleeve that the yarn started from, keeping the needle horizontal; come through the work two bars along to the left.

4 Continue to work in this way, but take three bars from the body every couple of stitches. This will ensure that the body and sleeve fit together evenly without stretching.

Grafting

This can be a useful technique when an invisible seam is needed, and when two fabrics are still on the needles.

1 Using the knitting yarn, work from right to left. From the back of the fabric, bring the needle through the first knitted stitch of the lower fabric, and through the first stitch of the upper fabric.

2 From the front, thread the needle back through the center of the first stitch on the lower fabric where the yarn leaves, then out of the center of the next stitch on the left.

 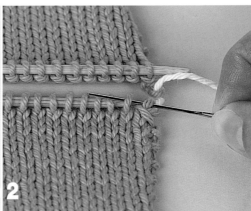

3 Thread the needle through the center of the top stitch and along the center of the next. Continue like this, and as each stitch is worked, keep slipping the knitting needle from them.

Whipstitch

This is a good stitch for attaching facings and fold-back hems.

Fold the hem, wrong sides together, making sure the stitches line up, and pin into place. Thread a needle and insert it through the loop created by a stitch on the wrong side of the fabric, and then through the center of the corresponding stitch on the bind-off edge. Bring the yarn through and repeat.

Picking Up Stitches

The patterns in this book break down the number of stitches needed to be picked up at each point of the neck to give an even finish.

1 Holding the needle in your right hand, insert it through the center of the first stitch from the front to the back.

2 Wrap the new piece of yarn around the knitting needle from back to front, as if to knit.

3 Pull the loop through the knitted stitch to the front.

When picking up stitches on a vertical edge, such as down the front or back of the neck, use this same method but pick up one stitch in from the edge.

Depending on the pattern instructions not every stitch will be required, so pick up stitches as evenly as possible to avoid stretching certain areas.

Attaching Collars

1 To attach a collar evenly and neatly, fold it in half, or count the knitted stitches to find the center. Pin this point to the center back neck, and join them together with a pin or basting stitch. Repeat this with the front edges each side.

2 To sew the collar to the body, thread a needle with enough yarn to sew the whole seam. Start at the center back. Bring half the length of yarn through and begin to sew the collar to the neck using a slip stitch or mattress stitch; when you have reached the center front, secure the yarn on the inside edge and then return to the center back to stitch the remaining side.

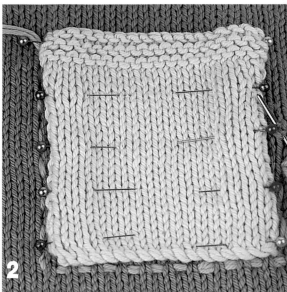

Attaching Pockets

1 Pin the pressed and blocked pocket to the main body. Use a running stitch in a contrasting color to mark the position of the pocket to guide you when attaching the two pieces. Make sure that the pocket runs in line with the stitches on the main garment. Use mattress stitch to invisible seam it into place.

2 The bottom edge of the pocket can be sewn into place using a stitch similar to a grafting stitch. Make sure that the stitch is worked through the pocket and the main knitted fabric.

B O D Y   1

CLASSIC CREW NECK

pocket

sleeve   *neckline*

sleeve

S L E E V E   1

FITTED SLEEVE

SIZES

	Small	Medium	Large
To fit bust in. (cm)	34 (86)	36 (91)	38 (97)
Actual size	36 (91)	38 (97)	40 (102)
Sleeve Seam Long	17 (43)	17 (43)	17 (43)
Sleeve Seam ¾	10 (25)	10 (25)	10 (25)
Sleeve Seam Short	4 (10)	4 (10)	4 (10)

MATERIALS

DK yarn

Jaeger Trinity. Shade 435

  6 50g balls (218 yds, 200 m per ball)

1 pair size 6 (4 mm) and size 5 (3.75 mm) needles

GAUGE

22 sts x 30 rows = 4 in. x 4 in. (10 cm x 10 cm) over stockinette stitch (st st) on size 6 (4 mm) needles or needles required to obtain this gauge.

ABBREVIATIONS

See page 125.

FRONT

Cast on 116 (122, 128) sts using size 5 (3.75 mm) needles.

Work 24 rows in k1, p1 rib.

Change to size 6 (4 mm) needles.

Work 10 rows in st st starting with a knit row.

Shape Body

1st row (RS) K3, SSK, k to last 5 sts, k2tog, k3.

Repeat this 1st row every 8 rows until 8 sts in total decreased on each side. 100 (106, 112) sts on needle.

Work straight for 18 rows.

Shape Armhole

RS facing. Bind off 2 sts at beginning of next 2 rows.

3rd row (RS) K3, SSK, k to last 5 sts, k2tog, k3.

Repeat this 3rd row every RS row until 25 sts in total decreased on each side. 50 (56, 62) sts on needle.

Shape Neck

1st row (RS) K3, SSK, k8 (11, 14) sts, place remaining 37 (40, 43) sts on a holder. Turn to work left side of neck.

2nd row (WS) Bind off 1 st, purl to end.

3rd row K3, SSK, knit to end.

Repeat these 2nd and 3rd rows until 6 sts in total decreased on neck edge.

Continue armhole shaping until 3 (6, 9) sts remain.

Work 2 rows. Bind off.

For a sleeveless option to this garment continue to work remaining sts after armhole decrease for a further 10 rows. Bind off. These can then be attached to the back of the garment section to form a thin strap.

RS facing. Rejoin yarn and bind off 24 sts from holder.

Work as for left side reversing all neck shaping and continuing armhole decrease over last 5 sts of each RS row.

For a sleeveless option to this garment continue to work remaining sts after armhole decrease for a further 10 rows. Bind off. These can then be attached to the back of the garment section to form a thin strap.

BACK

Cast on 116 (122, 128) sts using size 5 (3.75 mm) needles.

Work 24 rows in k1, p1 rib.

Change to size 6 (4 mm) needles.

Work 10 rows in st st starting with a knit row.

Shape Body

1st row (RS) K3, SSK, k to last 5 sts, k2tog, k3.

Repeat this 1st row every 8 rows until 8 sts in total decreased on each side. 100 (106, 112) sts on needle.

Work straight for 18 rows.

Shape Armhole

RS facing. Bind off 2 sts at beginning of next 2 rows.

3rd row (RS) K3, SSK, k to last 5 sts, k2tog, k3.

Repeat this 3rd row every RS row until 30 sts in total decreased on each side. 40 (46, 52) sts on needle.

Shape Neck

1st row (RS) K7 (10, 13) sts, place remaining 33 (36, 39) sts on a holder. Turn to work right side of neck.

2nd row (WS) Bind off 1 st, purl to end.

Repeat this 2nd row on every WS row until 4 sts in total decreased on neck edge. 3 (6, 9) sts remain.

Work 1 row. Bind off.

RS facing. Rejoin yarn and bind off 26 sts from holder.

2nd row (WS) Purl.

3rd row Bind off 1 st, knit to end.

Repeat this 3rd row on every RS row until 4 sts in total decreased on neck edge. 3 (6, 9) sts remain.

Work 1 row. Bind off.

MATERIALS

DK yarn

Rowan Wool and Cotton. Shade 901

  1 50g ball (123 yds, 113 m per ball)

1 pair size 5 (3.75 mm) needles

GAUGE

22 sts x 30 rows = 4 in. x 4 in. (10 cm x 10 cm) over stockinette stitch (st st) on size 6 (4 mm) needles or needles required to obtain this gauge.

ABBREVIATIONS

See page 125.

POCKET BAGS (Make 2)

Cast on 38 sts using size 5 (3.75 mm) needles.

Work in st st starting with a knit row.

Work for 80 rows.

RS facing. Bind off.

Fold the knitting RS together so that the cast-on and cast-off edges meet. Stitch together leaving one side open.

Position the pocket bags approximately ¾ in. (2 cm) above the hem finish on the front of the garment. The bags will be attached to the side seams. Stitch the back of the pocket bag to the back side seam and place the front of the pocket bag to the front side seam.

Pocket Border

RS facing. With the front side seam of garment and front of pocket bag together, pick up 30 sts along edge and work in seed stitch.

1st row (WS) * P1, k1, repeat from * to end.

2nd row (RS) * K1, p1, repeat from * to end.

Repeat these two rows twice then 1st row once more. 7 rows worked in all.

RS facing. Bind off in seed stitch.

Stitch down the seed stitch to the side of the garment to give a neat finish.

Any stitch pattern can be substituted for the pocket edge pattern above. Use any detail or pattern set-up used on hems or collars to complement the detailing already used on the main body of the garment.

SHOWCASE

THE FOLLOWING PAGES SHOW A SELECTION OF THE FINISHED
GARMENTS THAT CAN BE CREATED USING THE MIX AND MATCH
SYSTEM. ALL GARMENTS ARE KNITTED TO THE SMALL PATTERN SIZE.

OVERSIZE SWEATER

YARN Rowan Wool and Cotton Shade 953
BODY 23 (page 84)
SLEEVE 14 (page 40) Work shaping as listed in pattern but echo
the stitch pattern from the main body. Use the center front of the
main body as the center of the sleeve and work stitch pattern
placement accordingly.
NECK 26 (page 94)
POCKET 4 (page110) Work as large size. Use the relief stitch pattern
of the main body, remembering to centralize the pattern. Work pocket
border as 1x1 rib to match hems.

LONG WRAP CARDIGAN

YARN as listed on page 52

BODY 14 *(page 52)*

SLEEVE 2 *(page 16)* With turnback cuff detail. The first 24 rows of the cuff were worked using the same rib stitch and cable repeat as the cardigan hem. The cable rows were worked on the reverse side so that the cables are visible when

the cuff is turned back. The remaining rows were worked as rib only.

NECK 1 *(page 44)* Follow the directions for the cardigan finish but without picking up the stitches from the front bands. Work in the stitch pattern repeat for the hems of the cardigan body. Remember to work cables on the reverse side of work

so that they are visible when the collar turns back.

BELT 2 *(page 102)* Use the rib stitch pattern repeat as for the hem for the first 24 rows and last 24 rows of the belt.

POCKET 4 *(page 110)* The detail on the panel echoes the hem detail of the cardigan.

SQUARE V-NECK

YARN as listed on page 106
BODY 29 *(page 106)*
SLEEVE 10 *(page 32)* Work the first 6 rows in contrast Yarn B to match hem detail of the body then follow the sleeve shaping as listed in pattern.
NECK 17 *(page 76)* Work in 2x2 rib. As an additional detail contrast Yarn B has been introduced in the central section of the neck band so that the contrast tipping color detail is echoed at the neck in addition to the hem and cuffs.
POCKET 1 *(page 104)* Large size worked in 2x2 rib.

SHORT FITTED SWEATER

YARN Rowan KidSilk Haze Shade 600 (Main Color) Shade 591 (Contrast color)
BODY 3 *(page 18)*
SLEEVE 1 *(page 14)* ¾ length. Work 24 rows in 1x1 rib to match the main body. Then work sleeve shaping as in the pattern.
NECK 3 *(page 48)*

FITTED CARDIGAN

YARN Jaeger Aqua Cotton DK Shade 320
BODY 8 *(page 30)* Longer length.
SLEEVE 1 *(page 14)* Long length. Use the same seed stitch for hem to match the main body.
NECK 1 *(page 44)* Follow directions for the cardigan finish. Work in seed stitch for 24 rows. Include 2 button spacings on the neck edge.
BELT 1 *(page 100)*
POCKET 3 *(page 108)* Work in seed stitch to match the hem details.
13 buttons.

WRAP CARDIGAN

YARN as listed on page 70
BODY 19 *(page 70)*
SLEEVE 1 *(page 14)* Long length.
Work hem in seed stitch to match the
stitch pattern of the tie hem finish.
NECK 14 *(page 70)*

BORDER PATTERN CARDIGAN

YARN Jaeger Matchmaker Merino DK Shade 887 (Main Color) Shades 880, 856 (Contrast Colors)

BODY 30 *(page 108)* Short length.

SLEEVE 9 *(page 30)* Work cuff using the hem pattern for the main body and work the Fair Isle border pattern from the chart, reversing Yarns B and C. Then follow the sleeve shaping instructions as listed in the pattern.

NECK 2 *(page 46)* Follow the directions for the cardigan finish. Work front bands in pattern as before, then work the neck band in 1x1 rib. Work for 24 rows.

FAIR ISLE CARDIGAN

YARN as listed on page 48

BODY 13 *(page 48)* Longer length.

SLEEVE 2 *(page16)* Without turnback cuff use the same 1x1 rib pattern to match the main body. One repeat of the Fair Isle detail from the body was used to echo the main body detail.

NECK 2 *(page 46)* Follow directions for cardigan finish. Work in 1x1 rib to match hem and cuffs of the main body and sleeves.

6 button spacings

BEADED SWEATER

YARN as listed on page 62

BODY 17 *(page 62)*

SLEEVE 1 *(page14)* Short length. Hem detail and beading pattern follows the main body patterning. Follow the graph for the beading placement. Use the center front of the main body as the center of the sleeve and work bead placement accordingly.

NECK 28 *(page 98)* Pick up stitches as in instructions. Work in a seed stitch to echo the body and sleeve hem detail.

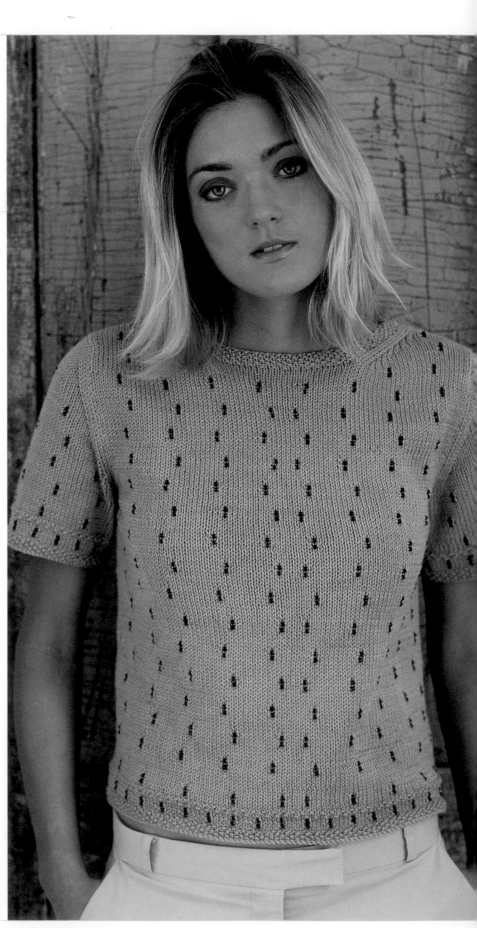

RIB AND EYELET CARDIGAN

YARN as listed on page 96
BODY 26 *(page 96)*
SLEEVE 9 *(page 30)* Use the same 1x1 rib pattern to match the hem detail on the main body. The knit and purl stitch relief pattern on the main body was echoed on the sleeve for additional detail.
NECK 1 *(page 44)* Follow directions for the cardigan finish. Spacing for a buttonhole on the neck edge was included.
7 buttons

USEFUL INFORMATION

This section gives information on the equipment you will need to make the garments, the abbreviations used in the patterns, and useful advice on yarn types and substitution.

MATERIALS AND EQUIPMENT

Yarn needles should have large eyes and blunt tips to prevent splitting strands of yarn.

Each pattern lists the equipment you will need to complete each project. However, there are several basic tools that may not be listed, but will be needed for all projects. These include a measure tape, a pair of scissors, a large-eyed blunt sewing needle, a sewing needle and thread, and some knitting pins. The knitting-needle size stated in each project is the same. However, it is extremely important that with each new yarn you use, a gauge swatch is knitted, as it may be necessary to go up or down a needle size.

Knitting needles come in a range of sizes. The patterns have been knitted using size 6 (4 mm) and size 5 (3.75 mm) needles, but you may need to use other sizes to knit to the correct gauge.

Sharp scissors

Knitter's pins have large heads to help you see them in the knitting.

Preisgruppe-catégorie de prix
price group ☐ I

INOX

mm		mm
		6
		6 1/2
2	Nadelmaß für	
2 1/4	Stricknadeln	7
2 1/2		
2 3/4		7 1/2
3	Knitting Pin	
3 1/4	Gauge	8
3 1/2		
3 3/4	Jauge pour	9
4	Aiguilles à	
4 1/2	Tricoter	
5		10
5 1/2		

You can check the size of your knitting needles with a needle gauge.

Bobbins hold small amounts of yarn, so are particularly useful for intarsia knitting.

Row counters

Point protectors are useful when storing or transporting work in progress.

NEEDLE CONVERSION CHART

U.S.	OTHER
19	15 mm
17	12 or 13 mm
15	10 mm
13	9 mm
11	8 mm
	7.5 mm
	7 mm
10½	6.5 mm
10	6 mm
9	5.5 mm
8	5 mm
7	4.5 mm
6	4 mm
5	3.75 mm
4	3.5 mm
3	3.25 mm
	3 mm
2	2.75 mm
	2.5 mm
1	2.25 mm
0	2 mm

ABBREVIATIONS

The following abbreviations have been used in the patterns in this book.

ABCD etc   contrasting colors as indicated in color key of patterns

approx   approximately

cm   centimeter

C2B   Slip 1 stitch onto cable needle and at back of work. Knit next stitch then knit stitch from cable needle.

C2F   Slip 1 stitch onto cable needle and hold at front of work. Knit next stitch then knit stitch from cable needle.

C3L   Slip next stitch onto cable needle and hold at front of work. Knit next 2 stitches, then knit stitch from cable needle.

C3R   Slip next 2 stitches onto cable needle and hold at back of work. knit next stitch then knit 2 stitches from cable needle.

C4B   Slip next 2 stitches onto cable needle and hold at back of work, knit next 2 stitches, then knit stitches from cable needle.

C4F   Slip next 2 stitches onto cable needle and hold at front of work, knit next 2 stitches, then knit stitches from cable needle.

in.(s)   inch(es)

K, k   knit

k2tog   knit two stitches together

k3tog   knit three stitches together

MB   move bead

mm   millimeter

P, p   purl

psso   pass slipped stitch over

RS   right side

sl   slip

ssk   slip slip knit

st(s)   stitch(es)

st st   stockinette stitch

WS   wrong side

yf   yarn forward

yo   yarn over

( )   repeat instructions inside brackets

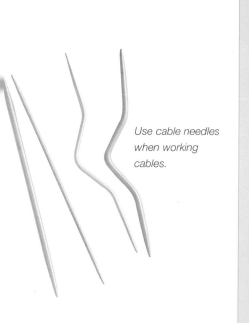

Use cable needles when working cables.

Circular needles can be useful for knitting necks.

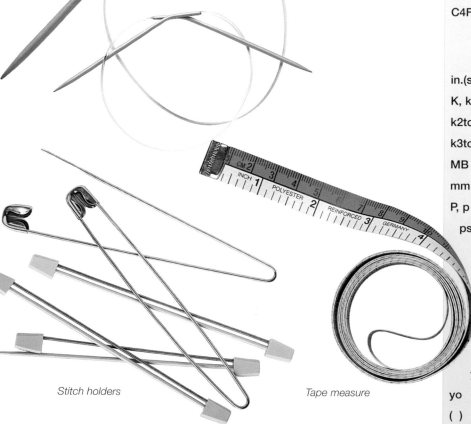

Stitch holders

Tape measure

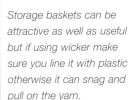

SUBSTITUTING YARN

Yarn choice is an important element in the design process, and it will determine the overall look and mood of your garment. Using a different yarn for the same project can have a dramatic effect on the appearance. Changing the color and type of yarn is an easy way to transform the finished look and make the garment unique.

The Rowan and Jaeger yarns used in this book all knit to the same gauge, but have very different properties, demonstrating how varied and flexible your design options can be. Each yarn fiber has a different characteristic, and this will alter the fabric effect and thus the personality of the garment. The following will help you to decide which yarn is the best for your needs. The designs featured in this book have all been knitted in yarns.

Yarn supplied in hanks must be wound into balls before knitting.

Wool (1)

Wool is the most commonly associated yarn with knitting, and it is a great, warm winter yarn. It is a very durable, versatile, and easy yarn to work with. It works particularly well for Fair Isle and intarsia color work techniques, as the fibers adhere and blend together well, and tend to prevent gaps from forming where the color change takes place. It is also generally spun with a smooth appearance, so is good for showing stitch detail, and its natural elastic property means it is good for ribs and cable fabrics that need to pull in.

Cotton (2)

Cotton is made from a natural plant fiber, and although historically used as a summer yarn, it is warm in the winter and cool in the summer. It generally has a smooth appearance, so it is good for showing stitch detail. Depending on how it has been finished, it can have a matt, mercerized, or glazed effect.

Wool and Cotton (3)

This yarn is a blend of both cotton and wool fibers. It is a good yarn choice for any season, and is a very versatile yarn for knitting and designing with. It is also particularly good for those who feel wool is too itchy, but like the comfort and elasticity that wool provides.

Storage baskets can be attractive as well as useful but if using wicker make sure you line it with plastic otherwise it can snag and pull on the yarn.

Silk and Cotton Mix (4)

This yarn blends two very different fibers: Silk, which is associated with luxury and tends to produce a good drapery fabric, and the crispness of the cotton. This is a good yarn for summer, and when it has a slubbed appearance it is useful at providing additional interest when knitting stockinette stitch. However, its non-elastic quality does mean it is not suited to clinging or stretchy stitch structures.

Mohair (5)

Mohair is often classed as a fashion yarn due to its highly personalized fabric surface. It can also be disliked by some as they feel it is too fluffy, and an irritant. Mohair is now often blended with other fibers to overcome this. The one used in this book is mixed with silk, and is very fine and discreet in appearance, giving it a refined and luxurious feel.

SUPPLIERS OF ROWAN YARNS

Rowan yarns are available from all good department stores. For further information call Rowan Yarns direct on: 01484 681 881 or visit their website: www.knitrowan.com

For information on suppliers outside the U.K., contact the Rowan distributor in your country:

Australia
Australian Country Spinners,
314 Albert Street
Brunswick
Victoria 3056
Tel: (03) 9380 3888

Canada
Diamond Yarn
9697 St Laurent
Montreal
Quebec H3L 2N1
Tel: (514) 388 6188

Diamond Yarn
155 Martin Ross, Unit 3
Toronto
Ontario M3J 2L9
Tel: (416) 736 6111
Email:
diamond@diamondyarn.com
www.diamondyarns.com

New Zealand
Alterknitives
PO Box 47961
Tel: (64) 9 376 0337

John Q Goldingham
PO Box 30 645
Tel (64) 4 586 4530

U.S.A.
Rowan USA
4 Townsend West, Suite 8
Nashua
New Hampshire 03063
Tel: (603) 886 5041/5043
Email: wfibers@aol.com

INDEX

Page numbers in italics refer to Showcase

CREDITS

The author would like to thank Jeff, family, and friends for all their support.

Many thanks to Sandra Brown, who has worked so hard producing so much knitting in such a short space of time, and to the other knitters, Wendy O'Shea, Kriss Morrison, and Diane Griffiths.

Special thanks Kate Butler at Rowan for the kind sponsorship of Rowan and Jaegar yarns.

Thanks also to Kate Kirby, Paula McMahon, Elizabth Healey, and all at Quarto who have helped in realizing this book

Quarto would like to thank Susannah Jose at Models Direct and Jackie Jones for hair styling and make up.

All photographs and illustrations are the copright of Quarto Publishing plc. While every effort has been made to credit contributors, Quarto would like to apologize should there have been any omissions or errors.